Why You Should
Read Children's
Books, Even
Though You Are
So Old and Wise

Books by Katherine Rundell

The Girl Savage
Rooftoppers
The Wolf Wilder
The Explorer
The Good Thieves

For younger readers
One Christmas Wish

KATHERINE RUNDELL

Why You Should Read Children's Books, Even Though You Are So Old and Wise

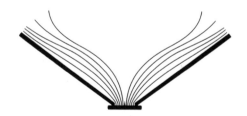

BLOOMSBURY PUBLISHING

LONDON · OXFORD · NEW YORK · NEW DELHI · SYDNEY

BLOOMSBURY PUBLISHING
Bloomsbury Publishing Plc
50 Bedford Square, London WC1B 3DP, UK

BLOOMSBURY, BLOOMSBURY PUBLISHING and the Diana
logo are trademarks of Bloomsbury Publishing Plc

First published in Great Britain in 2019 by Bloomsbury Publishing Plc

A catalogue record for this book is available from the
British Library

ISBN: HB: 978-1-5266-1007-2; eBook: 978-1-5266-1006-5

4 6 8 10 9 7 5

Typeset by RefineCatch Limited, Bungay, Suffolk
Printed and bound in Great Britain by CPI Group (UK) Ltd,
Croydon CR0 4YY

To find out more about our authors and books visit
www.bloomsbury.com and sign up for our newsletters

Why you should read children's books

The place I loved most as a child was the public library in Mount Pleasant, Harare, Zimbabwe. The children's section had seemingly not been restocked since the 1950s, and it smelt of the leaking roof and the ferocious sun which flooded, impeded only by dust, through the glass doors. The spines of the books were sun-bleached, and some had been taken out so rarely the fines on the returns slip were listed in shillings. It was there that I read my way through almost every book on the two dozen shelves: shelves which contained profoundly unlikely adventures, an enormous quantity of mediocre horse stories, and a book which had been shelved there by mistake in which the heroine has sex in a gondola. And, too, some of the greatest fiction ever written for anyone of any age at all.

Children's fiction has a long and noble history of being dismissed. Martin Amis once said in an interview: 'People ask me if I ever thought of writing a children's book. I say, "If I had a serious brain injury I might well write a children's book."' There is a particular smile that some people give when I tell them what I do – roughly the same smile I'd expect had I told them I make miniature bathroom furniture out of matchboxes, for the elves. Particularly in the UK, even when we praise, we praise with faint damns: a quotation from the *Guardian* on the back of Alan Garner's memoir *Where Shall We Run To?* read: 'He has never been just a children's writer: he's far richer, odder and deeper than that.' So that's what children's fiction is not: not rich or odd or deep.

I've been writing children's fiction for more than ten years now, and still I would hesitate to define it. But I do know, with more certainty than I usually feel about anything, what it is not: it's not exclusively for children. When I write, I write for two people: myself, age twelve, and myself, now, and the book has to satisfy two distinct but connected appetites. My twelve-year-old self wanted autonomy, peril, justice, food, and above all a kind of density of atmosphere into which I could step and be engulfed. My adult self wants all those things, and also: acknowledgements of fear, love, failure; of the rat that lives within the human heart. So what I try for when I write – failing often, but trying – is to put down in as few words as I can the things that I most urgently and desperately want children to know and adults to remember. Those who write for children are trying to arm them for the life ahead with everything we can find that is true. And perhaps, also, secretly, to arm adults against those necessary compromises and necessary heartbreaks that life involves: to remind them that there are and always will be great, sustaining truths to which we can return.

There is, of course, 1 Corinthians 13: 'Now that I have become a man, I have put away childish things.' But the writing we call children's fiction is not a childish thing: childish things include picking your nose and eating the contents, and tantruming at the failure to get your own way. The 45th President of America is childish. Children's fiction has childhood at its heart, which is not the same thing. Children's fiction is not written *by* children; it stands alongside children but is not of them.

(That children's fiction isn't written by children is probably for the best. I completed my first novel when I was about eight years old, as a birthday present for my father. I sewed a cover for it in blue silk and embroidered it with stars. It was called *Sally's Surprise*. The titular surprise, I find on rereading it, is presumably that there was no plot. Nothing happens. It was, in this sense, avant-garde and *Waiting for Godot*-esque. It had, though, a *lot* of descriptions of horses, which is less so.)

There is, though, a sense among most adults that we should only read in one direction, because to do otherwise would be to regress or retreat: to de-mature. You pass Spot the Dog, battle past that bicephalic monster PeterandJane; through Narnia, on to *The Catcher in the Rye* or Patrick Ness, and from there to adult fiction, where you remain, triumphant, never glancing back, because to glance back would be to lose ground.

But the human heart is not a linear train ride. That isn't how people actually read; at least, it's not how I've ever read. I learned to read fairly late, with much strain and agonising until, at last and quite suddenly, the hieroglyphs took shape and meaning: and then I read with the same omnivorous un-scrupulosity I showed at mealtimes. I read *Matilda* alongside Jane Austen, Narnia and Agatha Christie; I took Diana Wynne Jones's *Howl's Moving Castle* with me to university, clutched tight to my chest like a life raft. I still read Paddington when I need to believe, as Michael Bond does, that the world's miracles are more powerful than its chaos. For reading not to become something that we do for anxious self-optimisation – for it not to be akin to buying high-spec trainers and a gym membership each January – *all* texts must be open, to all people.

The difficulties with the rule of readerly progression are many: one is that, if one followed the same pattern into adulthood, turning always to books of obvious increasing complexity, you'd be left ultimately with nothing but *Finnegans Wake* and the complete works of the French deconstructionist theorist Jacques Derrida to cheer your deathbed.

The other difficulty with the rule is that it supposes that children's fiction can safely be discarded. I would say we do so at our peril, for we discard in adulthood a casket of wonders which, read with an adult eye, have a different kind of alchemy in them.

*

W.H. Auden wrote: 'There are good books which are only for adults, because their comprehension presupposes adult experiences, but there are no good books which are only for children.'

I am absolutely not suggesting adults read *only*, or even primarily, children's fiction. Just that there are some times in life when it might be the only thing that will do.

A caveat

There are of course many books marketed for children which wouldn't repay adult attention; these are often books which rely for their power largely on fart jokes, on the sheer tantalising fact of dinosaurs and on the physical gorgeousness of fairies. I certainly don't want to dismiss the ancient power of the fart joke – there are fart jokes dating back to 1900 BC – but I'm interested, here, in the texts for children that acknowledge the right of the child to have as rich a story as the adult writing it would demand for themselves. Not only the classics: there are such riches of new work every year. Children will not be patient if you pontificate or meander or self-congratulate. Rather, children's fiction necessitates distillation: at its best, it renders in their purest, most archetypal forms hope, hunger, joy, fear. Think of children's books as literary vodka.

On reading as a child

What is it like to read as a child? Is there something in it – the headlong, hungry, immersive quality of it – that we can get back to? When I was young I read with a rage to understand. Adult memories of how we once read are often de-spiked by nostalgia, but my need for books as a child was sharp and urgent, and furious if thwarted. My family was large, and reading offered privacy from the raucous, mildly unhinged panopticon that is living with three siblings: I could be sitting alongside them in the car, but, in fact, it was the only time when nobody in the world knew where I was. Crawling through dark tunnels in the company of hobbits, standing in front of oncoming trains waving a red flag torn from a petticoat: to read alone is to step into an infinite space where none can follow.

As a result I suffered from the bookworm's curse of knowing the meaning of words without knowing their pronunciation, never having heard them out loud. I pronounced *saccharine* wrong well into my twenties. I'm still not entirely sure about *pedagogy*. There were also words whose pronunciation was straightforward but whose meaning I did not know, and slowly pieced together from their surroundings.

I got a lot wrong: somnambulistic (P.G. Wodehouse: not a deadly illness), soporific (Peter Rabbit: nothing to do with lettuces). A fowling-piece in *The Wolves of Willoughby Chase* turned out to be a gun, and not, as I had assumed, some kind of weaponised bird. As a child, reading alone for the first time, I navigated a book like an unknown land in which unfamiliar words crop up like strange herbs, to be gathered now or stepped over and returned to later.

Martin Amis, expanding on his brain-injury comment, said: 'I would never write about someone that forced me to write at a lower register than what I can write'; but that's a total misunderstanding of what is at work in a children's book. I don't rein in the English language when I write, not because I expect all children to know every word, but because I trust that they're able to deduce or ignore the meaning without it collapsing the story. Francis Spufford, in his brilliant memoir *The Child That Books Built*, cites the research of Claude Shannon in 1948: Shannon, a mathematician working for the Bell Telephone Company, wanted to know how much of a telephone conversation could be lost to static before communication became impossible. He concluded that up to fifty per cent of a conversation or text could be either missing entirely or not understood before meaning becomes lost. Taking my cue from Shannon's *Mathematical Theory of Communication*, I've just finished the edit of my most recent children's novel. I've kept *facade*, *abundance* and *renunciation*, because there aren't other words that will do the same jobs of meaning, tone and rhythm so well. But the rule isn't a hard and fast one: I cut *adamantine*, a word I love and think children might also love, because it came at the climax of the story and I didn't want to lose even that split-second flicker of time that comes when a reader jumps over an unknown word. I would do the same if I were writing for adults.

On how children's fiction came to be

To love a thing – which I am, propagand-
istically and self-servingly, hoping to
persuade you to do – you must first know
both what it is, and how it got there. How,
then, did children's fiction come to be?

The first children's books in English were
instruction manuals for good behaviour.
My favourite, and the sternest in tone, is
The Babees' Book, which dates in manuscript
from around 1475: 'O Babees young,'
writes the author, 'My Book only is made
for your learning.' The text is a monu-
mental list of instructions in verse form:
'Youre nose, your teethe, your naylles,

from pykynge / Kepe at your mete, for so techis the wyse.'

In 1715, Isaac Watts published his fantastically uncheerful *Divine and Moral Songs for Children*. I find this book fascinating because its author's preface shows that the idea that it was intellectually degrading to write for children was strong by the eighteenth century: Watts writes, 'I well know that some of my particular friends imagine my time is employed in too mean a service while I write for babes ... But I content myself with this thought, that nothing is too mean for a servant of Christ to engage in, if he can thereby most effectually promote the kingdom of his blessed Master.' The book itself fits into the category, popular at the time, of 'upliftingly lugubrious'; it is largely made up of briskly invigorating rhymes about the inevitability of death:

Then I'll not be proud of my youth
    or my beauty,
Since both of them wither and fade;
But gain a good name by well doing
    my duty:
This will scent like a rose when I'm
    dead.

In 1744 came what's often called the first work of published children's literature, John Newbery's *A Little Pretty Pocket-Book, Intended for the Instruction and Amusement of Little Master Tommy and Pretty Miss Polly. With Two Letters from Jack the Giant-Killer; as also a Ball and Pincushion; The Use of which will infallibly make Tommy a good Boy, and Polly a good Girl*. Newbery's text is actually wittier than it sounds, shot through with a vein of irony, but its ancestry was clear: it came from a history of pedagogical* texts and situated itself among them. Newbery's text set a pattern: children's books would be instructive first and entertaining second.

---

* I do not know how to pronounce this word.

Alongside the morally uplifting accounts of Sunday schools and rigorously unpicked noses, though, there was another kind of story evolving, of a more unruly and subversive kind: the fairytale.

On wild hungers and heroic optimism

Fairytales were never just for children. They are determinedly, pugnaciously, for everyone – old and young, men and women, of every nation. Marina Warner argues that fairytales are the closest thing we have to a cultural Esperanto: whether German, Persian, American, we tell the same fairytales, because the stories have migrated across borders as freely as birds.

All fairytales, by and large, have the same core ingredients: there will be the archetypal characters – stepmothers, powerful kings, talking animals. There will be injustice or conflict, often gory and

extravagant, told in a matter-of-fact tone
that does nothing to shield children or
adults from its blunt bloodiness. But there
will also usually be something – a fairy
godmother, a spell, a magic tree – which
brings the miracle of hope into the story.
'Fairytales,' Warner writes, 'evoke every
kind of violence, injustice and mischance,
but in order to declare it need not
continue.' Fairytales conjure fear in order
to tell us that we need not be so afraid.
Angela Carter saw the godmother as short-
hand for what she calls 'heroic optimism'.
Hope, in fairytales, is sharper than teeth.

That spirit of heroic optimism –
optimism blood-covered and gasping, but

still optimism – is the life principle writ large. It speaks to us all: because fairytales were always designed to be a way of talking to everyone at once. They provide us with a model for how certain kinds of stories – by dealing in archetypes and bass-note human desires, and in metaphors with bite – can yoke together people of every age and background, luring us all, witch-like, into the same imaginative space.

Fairytales are also a way of tracing our cultural evolution. More than any other kind of story, they live and breathe and change. *Cinderella* is a good example. It's the first fairytale I remember loving, long before I could read, perhaps because it's the most physically dynamic. In a squadron of sleepers (Snow White, Sleeping Beauty) and captives (Rapunzel, the unnamed spinner in Rumpelstiltskin), Cinderella was the one who did the most running, albeit mostly away from things, and in glass high heels.

The earliest known version of the Cinderella story dates from around 7 BC, an oral tale recorded by the Greek geographer Strabo in his *Geographica*. Those who are perplexed by the precedence that footwear takes over personality in the modern *Cinderella* would find the Strabo version even more so, for in it, the shoe precedes the woman: an eagle snatches a leather sandal from a beautiful woman and drops it into the lap of the king of Memphis (it's been pointed out to me I should clarify: the ruler of the ancient capital of Aneb-Hetch, rather than Elvis). The king is so moved by the exquisite shape of the sandal that he orders men to search the country for its owner, and makes her his wife.

It was Charles Perrault in his *Histoires ou Contes du Temps Passé* in 1697 who added the fairy godmother and the loco-motive pumpkin. In the Brothers Grimm 1812 version of *Cinderella*, *Aschenputtel*, the stepsisters cut off their toes and chunks of their heels in a bid to fit the slipper. One by one, the prince is fooled and embraces them, but the trick fails when the shoe overflows with blood. In Giambattista Basile's *La Gatta Cenerentola*, Zezolla, once married to the prince, offers the stepmother a trunk full of wonderful clothes; when she leans in, Zezolla slams down the lid, decapitating her. (I tell this story to children when I visit schools, and their joyful, riotous approval shakes the walls.) In her 1893 *Cinderella*, Marian Roalfe Cox compiled 345 variants of the nearly archetypal story: in the Icelandic version, the evil stepmother is an ogress, who makes her ogress daughter cut off her toes to deceive the prince. The prince finds out, kills the ogress daughter, makes porridge of her and feeds her to the hungry stepmother.

So fairytales have always evolved. Currently, though, in Britain, the princess narratives are anchored primarily by the Disney films (the earliest of which, *Snow White and the Seven Dwarfs*, dates from 1937); films which are marketed squarely at young, usually female, children. They have made us believe that fairytales are only for the young and beribboned. The market cap of Disney is currently around $200 billion; more than the GDPs of Iceland, Morocco, Namibia and

Kyrgyzstan put together. They make a colossal profit from telling those stories; they have a huge financial incentive to keep their versions foremost in the public eye. There are retellings published every year, but they haven't yet shifted our sense of the cultural authority of the stories in the Disney renderings; they're read as 'para-texts': texts that offer twists on the dominant narrative, rather than replacing it. And the dominant narrative will always, to an extent, be taken as having our cultural benediction behind it. As Spufford writes, 'we cannot be told "once there was a prince" without also being told (on some level and in some part) that it was right that there was a prince. What knits together out of nothing, and yet is solid enough to declare that it is so, recommends itself to us … In this lies the power, and the danger, of stories.'

If stories have the power to do good, they can presumably also do the opposite. I don't – before the *Daily Mail* unleashes itself at me – want to ban Disney or Cinderella. (A headline from 2017: 'At last we're united – by [that is, rallying furiously against] a mum trying to ban Sleeping Beauty'). Cinderella is a fantastically strange and remarkable story and if I had a child I would tell it to them. But the Disney Cinderella – the Cinderella who waits patiently to be seen, beautified, and chosen and made rich – not only lacks agency: she lacks *hunger*.

Real fairytales are about hunger: hunger for power, above all; but also hunger for justice, for love, for change and transformation, for other humans. Characters devour one another, sometimes literally, until they're stacked inside each other like Russian dolls. So if I had kids I'd like to tell the Disney *Cinderella* as one of many old versions, along with *La Cenerentola* and the Icelandic version: as part of a raucous and wild tradition. And I would like to tell, too, a new version: one in which Cinderella does even more running,

less waiting; one in which the heroic optimism remains but perhaps comes from
Cinderella herself: she could, metaphoric-
ally or possibly literally, devour her fairy
godmother.

It's not strange to want to change these
stories. These stories have always changed:
it would be strange to want to keep them
in stasis. As Angela Carter wrote, 'I am all
for putting new wine in old bottles, espe-
cially if the pressure of the new wine makes
the old bottles explode.' Fairytales, myths,
legends: these are the foundations of
so much, and as adults we need to keep
reading them and writing them, repossess-
ing them as they possess us.

On children's fiction today

It was in the middle of the nineteenth century, as paper became more affordable and childhood literacy rates soared, that children's fiction began to take the actual desires of children into account. The subversive hunger of fairytales, unleashed into the newly booming printing press, made its way into children's novels. Stories designed for children were unhitched from the schoolroom and the pulpit, and the First Golden Age of children's books was born. Lewis Carroll, Rudyard Kipling, J.M. Barrie and E. Nesbit killed the parents, or abandoned them, or left them when they fell or flew to Wonderland or Neverland, and in so doing they released the child from the imperatives of the adult world. It must have felt like dynamite. Orphaned and unsupervised children roamed through Storyland, wreaking the chaos necessary for an adventure to take place. Larger and wilder experiences were on offer: stories which pushed back at the edges of what was possible.

It was here that the idea that children were sweet or gentle or necessarily more simple or likeable than other kinds of humans was jettisoned, along with the idea that all logic must be adult logic. As a child, I had no illusions that children were sweet:

children, I knew from my own furious heart, were frequently nasty, brutish and short. In casting aside that idea, children's books began to play by their own rules and, in so doing, became works of art distinct in themselves, in their own tradition, not watered-down versions of some other, adult thing.

And that tradition has held. You could draw a family tree from Peter Pan, who first appeared in 1902 ('and thus it will go on, so long as children are gay and innocent and heartless'); to Mary Poppins in 1934, with her stern and impenetrable enchantments ('Mary Poppins never explains anything'); to the anarchic and surreal logic of *Where the Wild Things Are* (1963) and *The Tiger Who Came to Tea* (1968), who 'drank all the water in the tap'. (I met Judith Kerr only once: she said that one of her publishers wanted her to change that line, because it was impossible and they were afraid the impossible would trouble children. I am very glad she kept it.) And on to Roald Dahl and Frank Cottrell-Boyce and Lissa Evans and to someone whose name we do not yet know, writing somewhere a story that will shake us in our collective shoes.

The family tree keeps growing. Children's fiction today is still shot through with exactly the same old furious thirst for justice that characterises fairytales: the wicked stepmother is beheaded by a trunk, Mrs Coulter in Philip Pullman's *The Amber Spyglass* (2000) falls eternally through a hole in the tissue of the universe. And, too, knitted closely into the need for justice, there is a related stance, the happier cousin of protective retribution: that of wonder. In a world which prizes a pose of exhausted knowingness, children's fiction allows itself the unsophisticated stance of awe. Eva Ibbotson escaped Vienna in 1934, after her mother's writing was banned by Hitler; her work is full of an unabashed astonishment at the sheer fact of existence. *Journey to the River Sea* (2001) has a kind of wonder that other kinds of fiction might be too self-conscious to allow themselves. So it's to children's fiction that you turn if you want to feel awe and hunger and longing for justice: to make the old warhorse heart stamp again in its stall.

Politics

A lot of children's fiction has a surprising politics to it. Despite all our tendencies in Britain towards order and discipline – towards etiquette manuals and school uniforms that make the wearers look like tiny mayoral candidates – our children's fiction is often slyly subversive.

Mary Poppins, for instance, is a precursor to the hippy creed: anti-corporate, pro-play. Mr Banks (the name is significant) sits at a large desk 'and made money. All day long he worked, cutting out pennies and shillings … And he brought them home with him in his little black bag.' Edith

Nesbit was a Marxist socialist who named her son Fabian after the Fabian Society; *The Story of the Treasure Seekers* contains jagged little ironical stabs against bankers, politicians, newspapers offering 'get rich quick' schemes and the intellectual pretensions of the middle class.

And the same is true across much of the world; it was Ursula Le Guin, one of the greatest American children's writers, who said this: 'We live in capitalism. Its power seems inescapable – but then, so did the divine right of kings. Any human power can be resisted and changed by human beings. Resistance and change often begin in art. Very often in our art, the art of words.' Children's books in the house can be a dangerous thing in hiding: a sword concealed in an umbrella.

Children's books are specifically written to be read by a section of society without political or economic power. People who have no money, no vote, no control over capital or labour or the institutions of state; who navigate the world in their knowledge of their vulnerability. And, by the same measure, by people who are not yet preoccupied by the obligations of labour, not yet skilled in forcing their own prejudices on to other people and chewing at their own hearts. And because at so many times in life, despite what we tell

ourselves, adults are powerless too, we as
adults must hasten to children's books to
be reminded of what we have left to us,
whenever we need to start out all over
again.

Imagination

Children's fiction does something else too:
it offers to help us refind things we may
not even know we have lost. Adult life is
full of forgetting; I have forgotten most of
the people I have ever met; I've forgotten
most of the books I've read, even the ones
that changed me forever; I've forgotten

most of my epiphanies. And I've forgotten, at various times in my life, how to read: how to lay aside scepticism and fashion and trust myself to a book. At the risk of sounding like a mad optimist: children's fiction can reteach you how to read with an open heart.

When you read children's books, you are given the space to read again as a child: to find your way back, back to the time when new discoveries came daily and when the world was colossal, before your imagination was trimmed and neatened, as if it were an optional extra.

But imagination is not and never

has been optional: it is at the heart of everything, the thing that allows us to experience the world from the perspectives of others: the condition precedent of love itself. It was Edmund Burke who first used the term 'moral imagination' in 1790: the ability of ethical perception to step beyond the limits of the fleeting events of each moment and beyond the limits of private experience. For that we need books that are specifically written to feed the imagination, which give the heart and mind a galvanic kick: children's books. Children's books can teach us not just what we have forgotten, but what we have forgotten we have forgotten.

Aristotle would agree (probably). In around 350 BC he defended the import-ance of *phantasia*; he argued that to lead a truly good life it was necessary to be able to wield fictions – to imagine what might be or should be or even could never be. Plato, who mistrusted poets and would have mistrusted children's novelists even more, would like nothing about this essay. But defy Plato.

Hope

One last thing: I vastly prefer adulthood to childhood – I love voting, and drinking,

and working. But there are times in adult
life – at least, in mine – when the world has
seemed blank and flat and without truth.
John Donne wrote about something like it:
'The general balm th'hydroptic earth hath
drunk, / Whither, as to the bed's feet, life
is shrunk, / Dead and interred.' It's in those
moments that children's books, for me,
do that which nothing else can. Children's
books today do still have the ghost of their
educative beginnings, but what they are
trying to teach us has changed. Children's
novels, to me, spoke, and still speak, of
hope. They say: look, this is what bravery
looks like. This is what generosity looks
like. They tell me, through the medium of

wizards and lions and talking spiders, that this world we live in is a world of people who tell jokes and work and endure. Children's books say: the world is huge. They say: hope counts for something. They say: bravery will matter, wit will matter, empathy will matter, love will matter. These things may or may not be true. I do not know. I hope they are. I think it is urgently necessary to hear them and to speak them.

And where to find them

In order to read children's books, of course, you must first be able to access them. This, which could and should be both easy and free, currently risks becoming neither.

My love of that sun-bleached Harare library had a baffled edge to it: it seemed too good to exist. Why didn't people steal the books? (They do, of course, but at a relatively low rate of attrition: around five per cent. The most stolen books tend to be sex-and-witchcraft-based: a poll in America found that two of the most stolen books in the country were *The Prophecies of Nostradamus* and *The Joy of Sex*.) Yet in a world which wasn't, in my short experience, known for giving something for nothing, libraries were giving one of the best things in the world for free.

The Times reported recently that since the turn of the decade in England more than £300 million has been slashed from library budgets. More than 8 million people are active borrowers from libraries; still more use the libraries' other services, like internet and book groups, and yet 700 libraries and book-lending services have been closed by councils since 2010. And – a fact that people outside of education or kids' fiction tend to find staggering – the government won't mandate libraries in schools: currently the only institutions required by law to have libraries are prisons. To which it's hard to say much that isn't unrepeatable in front of children.

I still find libraries astonishing; I still think they speak to our better instincts. The library remains one of the few places in the world where you don't have to buy anything, know anyone or believe anything to enter in. It's our most egalitarian space. And we live in a world in which the problems that threaten to engulf us, surely, have inequality – and the catastrophes that inequality inflicts on men, women and children – at their heart. In these dustbin-fire days, to turn away from the institution of the library feels criminal. If hope is a thing with feathers, then libraries are wings.

The galvanic kick of children's books

In 2016, my understanding of the world I lived in was upturned: by Brexit, Trump, a sweep across Europe towards nationalism and insularity, terrorist attacks. In the immediate aftermath, adult literary fiction did not help: I couldn't make it work. It was reading through the prism of children's fiction that brought back my faith in what books can do: because what helped were the old narratives, told for the benefit of children and adults and anyone who would listen: Icelandic folk tales, Grimm. They said that this, though it felt like an ending, was not: there has always been vaunting ambition, bitter acrimony, misunderstanding, hunger for power, folly, kindness, passion. Fairytales have already recorded, in their sideways way, all of human vice and yet not fallen silent in despair.

I still believe – most days, most of the time – that stories have power. I believe, like Aristotle, that fiction can put forward truths, via narration, which cannot be baldly stated by abstract theoretical language. There are ideas in *Alice's Adventures in Wonderland* that I could no more summarise than I could sing you all the parts of a hundred-instrument symphony: fiction resists reduction. Fiction can't, by itself, right the world. But I believe, still, in the wild and immeasurable value of pouring everything you think good or important into a text, that another may draw it out again: what Elena Ferrante calls 'a fishing net that captures daily experiences, holds them together imaginatively, and connects them to fundamental questions about the human condition'. But if its value is to be maintained now, in this moment we're living in, when astonishing technological breakthroughs meet vast human inequality, we shall need new voices.

Kazuo Ishiguro said in his Nobel Prize address: 'We must search more energetically to discover the gems from what remain today unknown literary cultures, whether the writers live in faraway countries or within our own communities.' And for that to work, he says, 'we must take great care not to set too narrowly or conservatively our definitions of what constitutes good literature.' In doing so we might find ourselves borne up in the hitherto silenced talent that has not yet found a way into the public sphere. There is so dazzlingly much to gain.

And Ishiguro's call applies not just to adult fiction but to children's too. Children's fiction needs to widen and change again, as it has widened and transformed before. Recently a study of children's fiction in the UK showed that only four per cent of books published in a year had any characters who were black, Asian or minority ethnic, but that 31.2 per cent of school children are from minority ethnic origins. Like most writers, I often go to visit schools and, when I do, I ask the children to help me write a story – I ask for character names, a boy and a girl. Many of the schools I go to are in South London, where I live, and more than half of the children in the classrooms will have English as a second language, but the names they suggest in those schools are always the same: Jamie, Harry, Lizzy – Anglo-Saxon names pre-owned by monarchs. Those are the kinds of names, we've been telling children, that heroes have.

This isn't to say that children need to see exact replicas of themselves in every story they read – fiction, in giving you a front-row seat to another person's heart, allows you to be male, female, armoured bear – but every child does urgently need to be able to find themselves *somewhere*. As the world transforms so swiftly, children's fiction needs new, ever-more-various stories, from all across this kaleidoscopic planet on which we stand – already it has begun, but we need more; new ideas, new mediums, from places and voices we've hitherto failed to listen to: new jokes, new riches. This is the time for another twist in its evolution: another Golden Age.

*

There will be many who would shame you for children's fiction beyond the bright line of your eighteenth birthday. Your embarrassment is expected, indeed anticipated by the market: the Harry Potter books were issued with an alternative grown-up cover, so that the old and serious needn't blush on the bus. But refuse to be shamed. Apart from anything else, it's good practice. There's a gorgeous scene in the 1949 black-and-white film *Adam's Rib*, when

Katharine Hepburn questions her secretary about the moral double standards of the day: her secretary, defensive, says: 'I don't make the rules.' 'Sure you do,' says Hepburn. 'We all do.' Shame requires your acquiescence. So rebel. Go to an independent bookshop and stride towards the books with bright colours on their spines.

Elizabeth Barrett Browning, who knew more about a great deal than most of us, wrote about her childhood reading in *Aurora Leigh*; about how she:

> read my books,
> Without considering whether they
> were fit

To do me good. Mark, there. We get no
    good
By being ungenerous, even to a book,
And calculating profits, – so much help
By so much reading. It is rather when
We gloriously forget ourselves, and
    plunge
Soul-forward, headlong, into a book's
    profound,
Impassioned for its beauty and salt of
    truth –
'Tis then we get the right good from a
    book.

So defy those who would tell you to be
serious, to calculate the profit of your

imagination; those who would limit joy in the name of propriety. Cut shame off at the knees. Ignore those who would call it mindless escapism: it's not escapism: it is findism. Children's books are not a hiding place, they are a seeking place. Plunge yourself soul-forward into a children's book: see if you do not find in them an unexpected alchemy; if they will not un-dig in you something half hidden and half forgotten. Read a children's book to remember what it was to long for impossible and perhaps-not-impossible things. Go to children's fiction to see the world with double eyes: your own, and those of your childhood self. Refuse unflinchingly to be embarrassed: and in exchange you get the second star to the right, and straight on till morning.

Acknowledgements

It seems very grand to have acknowledgements for such a short text, but I want to note that I have shamelessly stolen ideas from many friends, particularly Liz Chatterjee, Amia Srinivasan and Sophie Smith. I owe thanks to Imogen Russell Williams, for the *Aurora Leigh* poem, and to Nick Lake, for sharing his ideas about the stern brilliance of Mary Poppins. Colin Burrow commented on a draft of this essay; I owe him a great deal for his immense and ongoing kindness. Cornelius Medvei is a very wise though not old person who reads children's books, and kick-started the idea.

And Charles Collier sent me a late-night email about the bite and glory of children's fiction from which I have made off, Aladdin-like, with many treasures.

An exciting adventure awaits!

Read on for a short extract

FLIGHT

Like a man-made magic wish, the aeroplane began to rise.

The boy sitting in the cockpit gripped his seat and held his breath as the plane climbed into the arms of the sky. Fred's jaw was set with concentration, and his fingers twitched, following the movements of the pilot beside him: joystick, throttle.

The aeroplane vibrated as it flew faster into the setting sun, following the swerve of the Amazon River below them. Fred could see the reflection of the six-seater plane, a spot of black on the vast sweep of blue, as it sped towards Manaus, the city on the water. He brushed his hair out of his eyes and pressed his forehead against the window.

Behind Fred sat a girl and her little brother. They had the same slanted eyebrows and the same brown skin, the same long eyelashes. The girl had been shy, hugging her parents until the last possible moment at the airfield; now she was staring down at the water, singing under her breath, her brother trying to eat his seatbelt.

In the next row, on her own, sat a pale girl with blonde hair down to her waist. Her blouse had a neck-ruffle that came up to her chin, and she kept tugging it down and grimacing. She was determinedly not looking out of the window.

The airfield they had just left had been dusty and almost deserted, just a strip of tarmac under the ferocious Brazilian sun. Fred's cousin had insisted that he wear his school uniform and cricket jumper, and now, inside the hot, airless cabin, he felt like he was being gently cooked inside his own skin.

The engine gave a whine, and the pilot frowned and tapped the joystick. He was old and soldierly, with brisk nostril hair and a grey waxed moustache which seemed to reject the usual laws of gravity. He touched the throttle and the plane soared upwards, higher into the clouds.

It was almost dark when Fred began to worry. The pilot began to belch, first quietly, then violently and repeatedly. His hand jerked, and the plane dipped suddenly to the left. Someone screamed behind Fred. The plane lurched away from the river and over the canopy. The pilot grunted, gasped and wound back the throttle, slowing the engine. He gave a cough that sounded like a choke.

Fred stared at the man – he was turning the same shade of grey as his moustache. 'Are you all right, sir?' he asked. 'Is there something I can do?'

Fighting for breath, the pilot shook his head. He reached over to the control panel and cut the engine. The roar ceased. The nose of the plane dipped downwards. The trees rose up.

'What's happening?' asked the blonde girl sharply. 'What's he doing? Make him stop!'

The little boy in the back began to shriek. The pilot grasped Fred's wrist hard for a single moment, then his head slumped against the dashboard.

And the sky, which had seconds before seemed so reliable, gave way.

About the Author

Katherine Rundell is the bestselling author of five children's novels and has won the Costa Children's Book Award, the Blue Peter Book Award and the Waterstones Children's Book Prize amongst many others. Her novels are now published in thirty countries. Katherine spent her childhood in Africa and Europe before taking her degree at the University of Oxford and becoming a Fellow of All Souls College. As well as writing, she studies Renaissance literature and is learning, very slowly, to fly a small aeroplane.